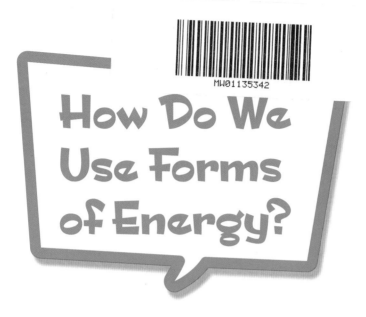

# How Do We Use Forms of Energy?

 HOUGHTON MIFFLIN HARCOURT

**PHOTOGRAPHY CREDITS:** COVER ©JFB/Stone+/Getty Images; 3 (b) ©Jupiterimages/Polka Dot/Alamy; 4 (b) ©Grady Coppell/Getty Images; 5 (bg) ©JFB/Stone+/Getty Images; 6 (b) ©Zuma Wire Service/Alamy Images; 7 (t) ©Corbis; 8 (b) ©David Frazier/Corbis; 10 (b) ©Jupiterimages/Getty Images; 11 (t) ©Westend61/Getty Images; 13 (t) ©Hemera Technologies/Getty Images; 17 (t) ©Stockdisc/Getty Images; 18 (b) ©GIPhotoStock/Science Source/Photo Researchers, Inc.; 19 (l) ©Jose Luis Pelaez Inc./Blend Images/age fotostock; 19 (r) ©Stockbyte/Getty Images; 20 (b) ©Cheyenne Glasgow/Flikr/Getty Images; 21 (t) ©Katharine Andriotis Photography, LLC /Alamy Images

Printed in Mexico

ISBN: 978-0-544-07315-9

4 5 6 7 8 9 10 0908 21 20 19 18 17 16

4500608014          A B C D E F G

# Be an Active Reader!

 **Look at these words.**

| | | |
|---|---|---|
| energy | chemical energy | conduction |
| potential energy | heat | convection |
| kinetic energy | thermal energy | radiation |
| mechanical energy | conductor | |
| electrical energy | insulator | |

 **Look for answers to these questions.**

What is energy?

What are the different forms of energy?

What causes sound?

What causes light?

Where does electrical energy come from?

What happens when fuels release chemicals?

What is heat?

How can energy change form?

How do objects react to heat?

How are conductors and insulators different?

How does an electric cord work?

How does heat move and change matter?

How do convection and radiation work?

## What is energy?

Look around your classroom. Energy is all around you. The lights are on because of energy. Energy heats and cools the building. The computers in the library use energy. You use energy, too!

You use energy in everything you do, whether it's writing, walking, running, playing a game—or even just talking. Energy is the ability to cause change in matter. Any type of movement is a change, so everything that moves has energy.

You use energy when you throw a ball.

## What are the different forms of energy?

Have you ever watched someone dive into a swimming pool? The diver raises her arms, bends her knees, and uses her feet to push off the board. She glides headfirst into the water.

It takes energy to dive. When the diver is standing, her body stores energy that is waiting to be used. Energy in this form is potential energy. It is the energy something has because of its position or condition.

When the diver pushes off and dives into the water, she is using kinetic energy. This is the energy of motion. The diver also uses kinetic energy when she comes back up to the surface of the pool, swims to the edge, and climbs out.

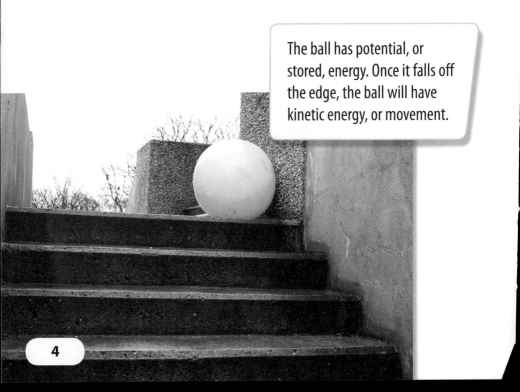

The ball has potential, or stored, energy. Once it falls off the edge, the ball will have kinetic energy, or movement.

This diver dives off a platform into the pool. The higher the platform, the more potential energy the diver has.

A diver standing on a platform has potential energy. This stored energy becomes kinetic energy when the diver jumps. The combination of potential and kinetic energy is called mechanical energy.

Once the diver moves off the platform, there is less potential energy. This is because the energy has changed to kinetic energy. As the diver moves toward the water, the amount of kinetic energy increases. The total amount of mechanical energy at any time is the sum of the potential and kinetic energy.

## What causes sound?

Did you know that energy causes sound? Sound is made when something vibrates, or moves back and forth. For example, when you pluck a string on a guitar, the string vibrates. These vibrations, or movements, make sound waves. The sound waves move through the air and reach our ears. We hear the sound waves as music.

Loud sounds have more energy than quiet sounds do. So, larger vibrations occur when sounds are loud. Pitch describes how high or low a sound is. A drum makes a low-pitched sound. A flute makes high-pitched sounds.

Dog parks have lots of barking dogs. Is the sound of barking dogs a loud or quiet sound?

What two sources of energy provide light in the photograph?

## What causes light?

Light is a form of energy that travels through space. Light energy is produced in different ways. The sun produces light. Then plants use the light from the sun to make food.

Electricity also produces light. Electricity brings light into our homes, schools, and other buildings. Electricity also brings light to outdoor spaces so that we can have sports events, outdoor concerts, and carnivals at night. Where else do you see lights at night?

## Where does electrical energy come from?

Electricity is also known as electrical energy, or energy that comes from an electric circuit. Anything that has to be plugged in to an electrical outlet, from a toaster to a refrigerator, uses electrical energy.

What happens when there is no electricity because of a storm? Homes have no light or heat. Businesses can't use their computers. Think of all the ways we depend on electricity.

Have you ever wondered where the electricity in your community comes from? In most places, energy-generating plants produce electricity. Energy-generating plants burn fuel, such as coal or natural gas, to produce electricity. In other places, the sun or the wind produces electricity.

Electrical energy brings light to the buildings in this city.

## What happens when fuels release chemicals?

When an electricity-generating plant burns fuel, a chemical reaction produces heat energy. Chemical energy is energy that is released by a chemical change. Chemical energy is changed into other forms of energy.

Our bodies store chemical energy. Experts remind us to eat a healthy breakfast every day. That's because food is our fuel. It provides the energy we need to study, work, and play sports.

When you turn on a flashlight, chemical energy is converted to light. The batteries in the flashlight store chemical energy. When you turn the switch, a chemical change takes place. The chemical change starts a flow of electrical energy that causes the light to shine.

Batteries provide energy for toys.

## What is heat?

Heat is the energy that moves between objects of different temperatures. It is the transfer of kinetic energy from one object to another. Thermal energy is the total amount of kinetic energy in a substance.

Imagine standing near a campfire. The heat from the fire feels warm because you are gaining heat energy. Heat moves from warmer objects to cooler objects.

When you boil water, you place a pot of water on a stove burner. Heat energy moves from the burner, which is hot, to the pot, which is cool. The pot gains heat energy, which then moves to the water. The difference in temperature between the burner and the pot is what makes the energy move.

This fireplace provides heat for a home. Heat energy moves from the burning logs to the cooler air in the room.

The heat from a volcano is extremely hot. The heat can reach 1,250 °C (2,000 °F)

Temperature is how hot or cold an object is. We measure temperature with a thermometer. Fahrenheit and Celsius are the two scales used for measuring heat. On the Fahrenheit scale, water boils at 212 °F and freezes at 32 °F. On the Celsius scale, the boiling point of water is 100 °C and the freezing point is 0 °C.

When temperatures drop to freezing or below, people wear warm clothing. Many animals have fur to keep them warm. In Antarctica, temperatures can be well below freezing—as low as –60 °C. The penguins living there huddle together. This way, they keep—and share—much of the heat energy their bodies produce.

## How can energy change form?

You've learned about several different forms of energy. Energy can change from one form to another. For example, when you sit still, potential energy is stored inside you. When you walk, run, or jump, the energy changes to kinetic energy, or motion.

Now picture logs burning in a fireplace. What do you see when you look at them? What do you feel when you stand near them? The logs contain chemical energy. When they burn, the chemical energy changes to light and heat energy.

When you rub your hands together, your hands get warmer. Kinetic energy changes to heat energy.

This alarm clock gets energy from batteries. The alarm rings when it's time to wake up. Chemical energy changes to electrical energy, which changes to sound energy!

There are many examples of how energy changes form.

- Switch on a light. Electrical energy flows through wires and then changes to light energy.
- Turn on a radio, a CD player, or an MP3 player and you hear music. Electrical energy flows through wires and changes to sound energy.
- Throw a ball to another player. Chemical energy in your body changes to kinetic energy.
- Stand at the starting line for the race. Potential energy changes to kinetic energy when you dash off toward the finish line.

Can you think of other ways energy changes form?

## How do objects react to heat?

Imagine sitting down on a metal chair that has been out in the sunshine. The chair will feel hot. Heat moves through some objects easily. A material that allows heat to move through it easily is called a conductor. Metals are excellent heat conductors. This makes metal a good material for pots and pans used for cooking.

In contrast to metal, glass is only a fair conductor of heat. If you pour boiling water into a metal bowl, the inside and outside of the bowl will heat up quickly. If you pour boiling water into a glass bowl, though, the inside of the bowl will heat up, but the outside of the bowl will not.

Pots and pans are made from metal because metal is a good conductor of heat.

Some materials are poor conductors of heat. Heat does not pass easily through plastic, rubber, or wood. Materials that don't conduct heat well are called insulators. A potholder is an insulator. It's made of materials that don't conduct heat well. That's why a potholder can protect your hand.

You've learned that metal is a good material for making pots and pans. However, if handles on a pot or pan are also made of metal, you can't pick up the pot when it's hot. That's why many metal pots have handles made of plastic or wood. Since these materials don't conduct heat well, they are insulators. They make the pot safe to pick up and hold.

Since wood is not a good conductor of heat, cooks often use wooden spoons to stir hot foods.

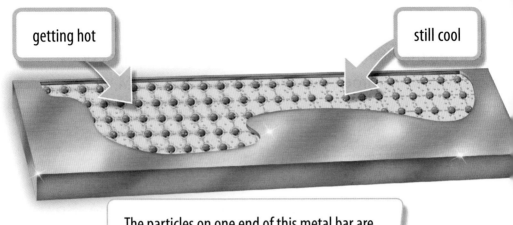

getting hot

still cool

The particles on one end of this metal bar are hot. That end was placed over a flame, but the other end wasn't. The particles on the other end aren't hot yet, but they will be soon.

## How are conductors and insulators different?

Many materials that conduct heat also conduct electricity. A good example is the metal copper. Copper wire is used to conduct electricity.

Heat insulators also work to insulate electricity. Materials such as plastic and rubber don't conduct electricity.

In general, solids are better heat conductors than liquids or gases are. That's because the particles in a solid are packed very close together. The particles move back and forth, but they don't move apart from each other. As a result, heat moves quickly from one particle to another.

How does fur keep an animal warm? Each thick hair is surrounded by air. The air and the fur act as insulators, keeping the animals warm.

Gases, on the other hand, are good insulators. One example of a good insulator is air. You may have heard that it's a good idea to wear layers of clothing when going outside in cold weather. That's because air becomes trapped between the layers. Each thin layer of air becomes a layer of insulation. The layers of air keep heat close to your body.

Insulators slow down the movement of heat. That's why insulators like plastic and rubber are used to cover the metal wires that conduct heat or electricity.

## How does an electric cord work?

Electricity provides energy for lamps and other household items. An electric cord attached to the lamp is plugged in to an outlet in the wall. There, a system of wires provides electricity.

An energy cord needs to conduct electricity and still be safe to touch. The cord is made of different types of materials. The material in the center of the cord is a conductor, such as copper wire. The wire carries the electrical energy from the power source to the lamp. The material outside the copper wire is an insulator, such as rubber or plastic. Since these materials don't conduct heat or electricity well, insulators make the electric cord safe to touch.

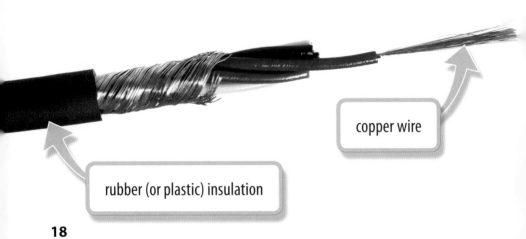

copper wire

rubber (or plastic) insulation

# How does heat move and change matter?

Heat can move from one material to another in three different ways: conduction, convection, and radiation.

Conduction is the movement of heat between two materials that are touching. Imagine walking barefoot on a sidewalk on a hot summer day. The heat moves to your feet because they are touching the hot surface of the sidewalk. Since your body is not as hot as the sidewalk, the heat is conducted to your cooler feet.

Next, imagine putting a frozen juice bar in your mouth. Your tongue immediately feels cold. Soon the juice bar begins to melt. The heat from your mouth begins to melt the juice bar.

Heat from a hot liquid in a cup warms your hands.

Your hands feel cold when touching an iced drink in a glass. Heat from your hands gradually warms the drink.

## How do convection and radiation work?

Convection is the transfer of heat within a liquid or a gas. Imagine heating a pot of soup over a campfire. First, heat moves from the burning logs to the pot. Then, the heat moves to the liquid in the pot. The liquid in the bottom of the pot gets warm. This warm liquid moves up to the top of the pot. The cooler liquid moves to the bottom of the pot. There, it heats up and moves back up to the top.

The movement of heat in the liquid continues as long as the pot of soup is heated. In this process, heat moves within the material, rather than from one material to another.

This pot of soup over a campfire shows the process of convection.

The heat from light bulbs warms the food without actually touching it.

Radiation is the movement of heat without matter to carry it. How can that happen? Think about a snowstorm. Snow covers the roads. Then the sun comes out. Heat from the sun melts the snow on the roads. But the sun itself doesn't touch the roads. Its heat does.

Radiation is perhaps the most important way that heat moves. Have you ever wondered how heat from the sun can reach Earth through the emptiness of space? There's no matter between the sun and Earth to carry the heat, so conduction doesn't explain it. And there's no liquid or gas in space, so convection doesn't explain it. The heat of the sun travels to Earth by radiation.

### Find the Best Insulator

Gather these materials: hot water, four glass jars, four rubber bands, aluminum foil, wax paper, plastic wrap, cotton fabric, thermometer, and a stopwatch or timer.

With adult supervision, pour hot water into each jar. Take the water temperature of each jar and record it in a table. Cover each jar with one of each material (aluminum foil, wax paper, plastic wrap, cotton fabric). Attach it with a rubber band. Predict which of the materials will be the best insulator. Set the stopwatch for 1½ hours. After that time, measure the water temperature in each jar and record. Which jar had the warmest water? Was your prediction correct?

### Research an Energy Scientist

Do research to learn about a scientist who has made contributions to the field of energy. Prepare an oral report about the work and contributions of this person. Include visuals that will help your audience understand more about the scientist and his or her discoveries.

# Glossary

**chemical energy** [KEM·ih·kuhl EN·er·jee] Energy that can be released by a chemical reaction.

**conduction** [kuhn·DUK·shuhn] The movement of heat between two materials that are touching.

**conductor** [kuhn·DUK·ter] A material that lets heat or electrical charges travel through it easily.

**convection** [kuhn·VEK·shuhn] The transfer of heat within a liquid or gas.

**electrical energy** [ee·LEK·trih·kuhl EN·er·jee] Energy that comes from electric current.

**energy** [EN·er·jee] The ability to cause changes in matter.

**heat** [HEET] The energy that moves between objects of different temperatures.

**insulator** [IN·suh·lay·ter] A material that does not let heat or electricity move through it easily.

**kinetic energy** [kih·NET·ik EN·er·jee] The energy of motion.

**mechanical energy** [muh·KAN·ih·kuhl EN·er·jee] The total potential and kinetic energy of an object.

**potential energy** [poh•TEN•chuhl EN•er•jee] Energy that an object has because of the object's position or its condition.

**radiation** [ray•dee•AY•shuhn] The movement of heat without matter to carry it.

**thermal energy** [THUR•muhl EN•er•jee] The total kinetic energy of the particles in a substance.